Mikaela Shiffrin

By Jon M. Fishman

AMAZING ATHLETES

Lerner Publications Company • Minneapolis

Lerner Publications Company
A division of Lerner Publishing Group, Inc.
241 First Avenue North
Minneapolis, MN 55401 USA

For reading levels and more information, look up this title at www.lernerbooks.com.

Library of Congress Cataloging-in-Publication Data

Cataloging-in-Publication Data for *Mikaela Shiffrin* is on file at the Library of Congress.
ISBN: 978–1–4677–5780–5 (LB)
ISBN: 978–1–4677–5782–9 (EB)

Manufactured in the United States of America
1 – BP – 7/15/14

TABLE OF CONTENTS

Mikaela Shiffrin competes in the 2014 Olympic Games,

YOUNGEST EVER

Mikaela Shiffrin gripped the handles of her ski poles. She bent her knees and leaned forward. With one big push, she was off and racing down the hill in the biggest skiing event of her life.

The 18-year-old skier from the United States

had a lot going for her. Mikaela had won the world championship in women's **slalom** in 2013. But the 2014 Olympic Games in Sochi, Russia, was her biggest test yet. She was competing against 59 women from around the world for a gold medal. Millions of people watched the race on television.

Slalom courses are full of twists and turns. Mikaela steers down this winding path with ease.

Slalom skiers must make tight turns around poles stuck in the snow. But they can't let the turns slow them down. Every fraction of a second counts in slalom races. Mikaela sped down the hill. She flew past pole after pole. She crossed the finish line with a great time.

Mikaela dodges poles on the slalom course.

Slalom events include two **runs** down the hill. Mikaela was in first place after the first run. But she was ahead by just 0.49 seconds. She was competing

Mikaela fights to beat the lead time in a race.

against former world and Olympic champions. Would she be able to keep her lead through the second run?

Since she was in first place, Mikaela would be the last skier to take her second run. Skier after skier zoomed down the hill. Many of the women improved on their first-run times.

Finally, it was Mikaela's turn to take her final run. She cruised down the hill. But then disaster almost struck. She was going too fast to keep her balance. One of her skis lifted off the ground, and she nearly crashed. "It scared me half to death," Mikaela said.

Mikaela stayed on her skis. Almost falling had slowed her down, though. She wasn't sure if she had gone fast enough to win.

The uncertainty ended when her time was announced. Mikaela had won the gold medal by 0.53 seconds! She had become

Mikaela looked happy and surprised after she won the gold!

the youngest skier to ever earn an Olympic gold medal in women's slalom at the Olympics. Reporters wanted to know how she felt. "It's hard to put into words how incredible this is," she said.

Mikaela also competed in the giant slalom in Sochi. She finished in fifth place. Giant slalom races are longer and sometimes steeper than slalom races.

Mikaela poses with the American flag after her big win in Sochi.

Mikaela (*front*) poses with her brother, Taylor, and her parents, Eileen and Jeff.

"FOLLOW ME"

Mikaela Shiffrin was born in Vail, Colorado, on March 13, 1995. Vail is a small town nestled in the Rocky Mountains. The area has some of the best ski slopes in the world.

The Shiffrin family loves to ski. Mikaela's father, Jeff, had skied for Dartmouth College in New Hampshire. His wife, Eileen, has been skiing since she was a young girl.

Together, Eileen and Jeff taught their kids to love skiing too. But the parents didn't pay for lessons for Mikaela and her older brother, Taylor. Instead, the kids learned from watching their mom and dad. "It was always 'Follow me' or 'Follow Mom,'" Jeff said. The family went out skiing together as often as possible. By the time Mikaela was in kindergarten, being on skis was second nature.

Mikaela's hometown of Vail, Colorado, is next to the third-largest ski mountain in North America.

Wind surfing was another sport Mikaela's family tried when she was growing up.

Skiing isn't the only sport the Shiffrins enjoy. When Mikaela and Taylor were young, they tried all kinds of activities, from **wind surfing** to soccer. But for Mikaela, nothing beat the rush of flying down a ski slope. "I love playing tennis and soccer, but skiing is definitely number one," she said.

The Shiffrins moved to Lyme, New Hampshire, in 2003. Jeff had found a new job at a hospital there. Mikaela was happy that there were plenty of places to ski near her new home. By the age of nine, she had decided her future was in skiing. At a summer ski camp that year, **instructors** asked the campers to write down a "Dream Goal." Mikaela wrote, "Be in the Olympics at age 16."

Mikaela's brother, Taylor, is on the ski team at the University of Denver.

The Dartmouth Skiway passes through Lyme, New Hampshire, where Mikaela moved when she was eight years old.

Mikaela had learned from her parents that the best way to become good at something was to practice as much as possible. Jeff believes that a person can master anything if he or she practices for at least 10,000 hours. Mikaela took her father's message to heart.

Mikaela and her mom finish a four-mile uphill run as part of Mikaela's training for the Olympics.

Mikaela trains both outdoors and indoors to get in shape for races.

PUSHING HERSELF

Mikaela began working with new focus to reach her Olympic dream. To get to 10,000 hours of practice, she split her time between skiing and working out in gyms. She also watched videos of **World Cup** skiers. She studied their **techniques** and tried to copy them on the hill.

Mikaela watched videos of Olympic skiers such as Julia Mancuso, who won the gold for giant slalom in 2006.

Mikaela enjoyed the hard work. "The more I trained, the more I liked to train," she said.

Before reaching the Olympics, Mikaela would have to prove herself in World Cup events. When she was 10 years old, she talked with her father about what she needed to do to reach the World Cup level. They decided Mikaela would have to work for five more years before she'd be ready for World Cup events. "And from that day, that was what I was going to do," she said.

Mikaela's brother, Taylor, was also chasing his skiing dreams. He went to school at Burke Mountain Academy in Vermont. The school is a place for young skiers to practice their sport while earning a high school **degree**.

Burke Mountain Academy was founded in 1970. Including Mikaela, 29 former Burke students have competed in Olympic Games.

In 2008, Mikaela also began studying and training at the school. All the practice began to pay off for Mikaela. She won race after race in 2008 and 2009.

Mikaela followed her brother to Burke Mountain Academy in the small town of Burke, Vermont (*right*), to train in skiing.

17

Her instructors at Burke were wowed by her skills. "For her age, she's the best I've ever seen," said **headmaster** Kirk Dwyer. But Mikaela's drive was even more impressive than her talent. "She doesn't want to know how great she is," Dwyer added. "She wants to know how she can improve."

In 2010, Mikaela skied in her first big international race. The Trofeo Topolino **alpine** skiing event takes place in Italy each year. Young racers from all around the world show up to compete. Mikaela blew past the other 14-year-old girls to win the slalom by 3.36 seconds. She also skied faster than any of the boys in her age group.

Besides the slalom and giant slalom, the three other Olympic alpine skiing events are downhill skiing, the super giant slalom (or super G), and the super combined.

Mikaela skis her first run of the 2011 FIS Alpine Ski World Cup women's slalom in Lienz, Austria.

ON TOP OF THE WORLD

After Mikaela's big victory in Italy, she started racing in Nor-Am Cup events. The Nor-Am Cup is a series of races for young skiers that takes place in North America. After racing in the Nor-Am Cup, many skiers go on to World Cup events.

Mikaela (*right*) took third place in the 2011 Audi FIS Alpine Ski World Cup. Marlies Schild of Austria (*middle*) took first, and Tina Maze of Slovenia (*left*) took second.

In 2011, Mikaela met the goal she set when she was 10 years old. She raced in a World Cup event at the age of 15. But she didn't make it onto a **podium** until her fifth World Cup race. At an event in Lienz, Austria, she finished third. Mikaela was thrilled with her bronze medal. "I have been working so hard for this moment," she said.

The third-place finish in Austria gave Mikaela confidence. She was the youngest woman to appear on a World Cup podium since 1978. She continued to ski well and was named World Cup **Rookie** of the Year for the season.

Then, in 2013, in her first full World Cup season, Mikaela began to win. She took first place in three slalom races before heading to the final event in Lenzerheide, Switzerland. If she could win there, she would be the overall World Cup slalom champion for the season.

Mikaela speeds downhill as she competes for the 2013 World Cup championship.

Mikaela's first run in Lenzerheide didn't go as well as she'd hoped. She was 1.17 seconds behind the leader, Tina Maze. But she nailed her second run. She rocketed down the **course** with the fastest time of the day. When Maze crossed the finish line in third place, Mikaela put her hands over her face and dropped to her knees. She was world champion!

"It's amazing," Mikaela said after the race. "I am still trying to find my best skiing but this was my best run of the season."

Mikaela raises her arms in celebration of her 2013 World Cup victory.

Mikaela stands on the alpine skiing training slopes at the Sochi 2014 Winter Olympics.

US HERO

Winning the slalom world championship in 2013 made Mikaela a household name among skiing fans. She was also becoming well known to people who didn't follow the sport closely. She appeared on the *Late Show with David Letterman* to talk about her championship.

She was photographed for the cover of *Sports Illustrated*'s preview issue for the Sochi Olympic Games.

The attention was fun for Mikaela. But her parents and Roland Pfeifer, her coach, worried that there was too much pressure on the young skier. The Olympics is the biggest

A sculpture of the Olympic Rings dominates this scene at the 2014 Winter Games in Sochi.

sporting event in the world. Mikaela had never competed in front of so many people before.

Mikaela seemed relaxed before the women's slalom event in Sochi. "In the morning she was really confident," said Coach Pfeifer. "That made me really comfortable." Mikaela soon showed why she was so confident, winning the Olympic gold medal despite almost crashing during her second run.

Mikaela poses with her coach, Roland Pfeifer, who was the world champion in slalom in 1992 and 1994.

Mikaela poses with her skiing gear in 2013.

The young gold medalist became even more popular after her victory in Sochi. Once again, she appeared on the cover of *Sports Illustrated*. This time, she had a gold medal around her neck. She was also featured on Wheaties cereal boxes.

Mikaela didn't spend much time celebrating her gold medal, though. On March 8, 2014, she was back on her skis to defend her world championship in women's slalom. This time, the race was in Are, Sweden. She won the event by 0.6 seconds for her second world championship in a row.

As the youngest women's Olympic slalom gold medalist in history, Mikaela has done a lot in a short time. But she says she's just getting started.

Mikaela heads for victory in the 2014 World Cup.

In fact, she's already planning for the 2018 Olympics, where she hopes to compete in all five alpine skiing events. "When I'm done I hope I can look back and say that I changed the sport," she said. "I do hope that I can inspire people to just ski their best, and don't be afraid to make mistakes because you'll learn from them."

Mikaela raises her World Cup trophy after becoming the women's slalom champion two years running.

Selected Career Highlights

2014 Won a gold medal in slalom at the Olympic Games
Named World Champion in slalom for the second time

2013 Won four World Cup slalom events
Named World Champion in slalom

2012 Won a bronze medal at the World Cup
Named World Cup Rookie of the Year

2011 Skied on the Nor-Am Cup series
Skied in her first World Cup event as a 15-year-old

2010 Skied in her first international ski competition

2008 Began school at Burke Mountain Academy
Began winning local races in her age group

2004 Decided she wanted to be an Olympic skier

Glossary

alpine: in high mountains

course: the path on a ski hill that slalom racers must follow

degree: a title given to a student after completing an area of study

headmaster: the person in charge of a school

instructors: people who teach skills

podium: the stand where the top three finishers receive their medals at Olympic and World Cup events

rookie: an athlete in her first year of high-level competition

runs: trips down the hill during a slalom race

slalom: a ski race down a winding path with poles to go around

techniques: methods of doing something

wind surfing: riding on a board with a sail on water

World Cup: the top level of international professional skiing

Further Reading & Websites

Bailer, Darice. *Ski Slopestyle*. Minneapolis: Lerner Publications, 2014.

Fishman, Jon M. *Gabby Douglas*. Minneapolis: Lerner Publications, 2013.

Meinking, Mary. *What's Great about Colorado?* Minneapolis: Lerner Publications, 2015.

Sports Illustrated Kids
http://www.sikids.com
The *Sports Illustrated Kids* website covers all sports, including skiing.

US Ski Team
http://usskiteam.com
The official website of the US Ski Team has recent news stories, statistics, biographies of skiers and coaches, and information about events.

Expand learning beyond the printed book. Download free, complementary educational resources for this book from our website, www.lerneresource.com.

Index

Photo Acknowledgments

The images in this book are used with the permission of: AP Photo/Luca
Bruno, p. 4; © Alain Grosclaude/Agence Zoom/Getty Images, p. 5; © Alexis
Boichard/Agence Zoom/Getty Images, p. 6, 21; © Clive Rose/Getty Images,
p. 7, 29; © OLIVIER MORIN/AFP/Getty Images, p. 8; © ALEXANDER KLEIN/
AFP/Getty Images, p. 9; © Imago sportfotodienst/Newscom/Newscom,
p. 10; © iStockphoto.com/Adventure_Photo, p. 11; © Bart Pro/Alamy, p. 12;
© Erin Paul Donovan/Alamy, p. 13; © Grant Hindsley/The Denver Post via
Getty Images, p. 14, 15; © THOMAS COEX/AFP/Getty Images, p. 16; © Andre
Jenny /Alamy, p. 17; © JONATHAN NACKSTRAND/AFP/Getty Images, p. 19;
© Christophe Pallot/Agence Zoom/Getty Images, p. 20; © FABRICE COFFRINI/
AFP/Getty Images, p. 22; AP Photo/Alessandro Trovati, p. 23; © Paul
Drinkwater/NBC/NBCU Photo Bank via Getty Images, p. 24; © Joe Scarnici/
Getty Images for USOC, p. 25; © Doug Pensinger/Getty Images, p. 26;
© Christophe Pallot/Agence Zoom/Getty Images, p. 27, 28.

Front Cover: © AFP/Getty Images.

Main body text set in Caecilia LT Std 55 Roman 16/28.
Typeface provided by Adobe Systems.